Couples & Sex

Bedroom Satisfaction that Works for Couples - Love Enhancer
through Intimacy

Grace Gary

Couples & Sex

INTRODUCTION

O n a rainy Sunday morning, Alex and Emily were enjoying an intimate moment while both were feeling incredibly aroused. The exchange started with a sensual shower massage and had now moved to the bedroom, where they had been engaged in lovemaking for the past ten minutes. Alex knew that Emily needed at least another five minutes of Intimacy before reaching her peak. However, there was a problem. Alex is uncertain if he could last another five minutes.

Continuing at the current pace, Alex knew that he might climax in a matter of seconds. He considered slowing down or stopping, but he also knew that any change in rhythm might frustrate Emily, who was at a stage where consistency was crucial. Moreover, stopping or changing rhythm could lead to a loss of erection, complicating matters further.

This dilemma was taking away from Alex's pleasure. While the initial moments had been exciting, he now felt worried and conflicted. It's hard to enjoy Intimacy when you're at odds with your own body. And when one partner can't fully enjoy it, the other can't either.

What Alex didn't realize was that he had another option: male multiple orgasms. A man who can experience multiple orgasms has incredible staying power. He doesn't have to hold back or fight his own body. He can enjoy all the sensations of lovemaking, reach a full climax, and continue without pause. He can last as long as his partner desires, experiencing excitement and release repeatedly. For such a man, the possibilities are limitless.

Alex isn't alone in having this option. Today, techniques exist to make multiple orgasms achievable for almost every man, regardless of age or experience. All it takes is the desire, one's own body, and a few minutes a day. So, don't stop here. Turn the page and discover a new dimension of your sexuality and a deeper connection with your partner.

Male multiple orgasms aren't just a physical feat; they can also enhance the emotional and spiritual aspects of Intimacy. By mastering these techniques, Alex can transcend the physical limitations of his body and experience a deeper, more fulfilling connection with Emily.

Imagine the joy and satisfaction of being able to fully satisfy your partner, knowing that you have the stamina and control to keep going as long as they desire. Male multiple orgasms can transform your sex life and take your relationship to new heights of Intimacy and pleasure.

In the following chapters, we will explore the techniques and practices that can help you become desirable for your partner. From understanding the male anatomy to mastering the art of arousal control, each chapter will provide you with the tools and knowledge you need to unlock your full potential in the bedroom.

Are you ready to embark on this transformative journey? Are you ready to experience the joy of satisfying your partner in bed and take your relationship to the next level? If so, let's begin. Turn the page, and let's start this incredible adventure together with this series of books.

Chapter 1

Satisfaction

Some people decide to live together first to see if they are able to adapt to each other's quirky ways. However, the elders do not always accept this, and neither is it condoned or encouraged. For whatever reason an individual decides to take on the journey of marriage, it should be done with caution and preparation to ensure a higher possibility of success.

The Basics

Trying to contribute equally to the marriage arrangement or relationship is essential, as both parties should understand that there is a part for each person within the marriage platform that should be taken seriously and without reservation.

The equality factor will significantly help to determine the commitment levels each individual is willing to contribute to the relationship in order to make sure it has a fighting chance of survival. There are many ways to ensure both parties stay participative in the marriage arrangement, and this would include being able to share all things, communicating well, being understanding and sensitive to each other's feelings and needs and many other positive contributing elements that will benefit the strength of the relationship.

Sometimes, when things don't go as well as intended, there may be a need to seek outside help to get things back on the upbeat track. This help may include the assistance of a counsellor, a marriage therapist or any other notable person whose primary function is to get the couple back into the mode where some positive progress can be made.

Sex is also another essential part of a successful marriage, and couples should understand the need to ensure this part of the marriage gets the adequate amount of attention it needs.

Making Fantasy a Reality

Every woman dream of a lover whose passion and stamina are so intense that he can last and satisfy her completely. Similarly, every man desires to fulfil these dreams, wanting to know that he can engage in lovemaking for as long as he wishes, bringing his partner to multiple climaxes. It sounds like an ideal scenario, but is it achievable?

In this book, you will discover the secrets of multiple male orgasms. By the time you finish reading, your understanding of sexual potential and power will be forever transformed. You will learn how to prolong Intimacy for as long as you and your partner desire. Men will learn how to master their bodies, experiencing complete and powerful orgasms without losing their erections and even achieving multiple orgasms, just like women.

I understand that this may seem hard to believe. It might seem like these sexual powers are only attainable by someone with unlimited energy, and extraordinary abilities or at the start of a passionate love affair. However, I assure you, these abilities are within reach for most men, regardless of age or relationship status.

You will be exposed to how to explore and enjoy sex in ways they never thought possible. I will show you that male multiple orgasms are not just fantasies from romance novels but a reachable reality. You will discover how being Mult orgasmic can enhance the pleasure and fulfilment you and your partner experience.

The ability to control one's erection and stay sexually active for extended periods is not limited to a select few. Many men have learned to control their erections in remarkable ways, experiencing multiple orgasms without losing their erections. These men are driving their partners wild with pleasure, and they're doing it consistently. These men are not sexual supermen; they are regular guys with varying characteristics and lifestyles. What they all share is the desire to please themselves and their partners, along with the discipline to master a simple technique.

I have personally witnessed some men become Mult orgasmic and increase their staying power. I have trained many of these men one-on-one, guiding them through the process. I can confidently say that every motivated man can master these techniques with dedication and practice.

If you are a woman reading this, be prepared for extraordinary surprises and pleasures. Whether you choose to actively participate in your partner's learning process or observe from the sidelines, your understanding of Intimacy with a man will be forever changed.

For men reading this, get ready to embark on a new relationship with your sexuality. The rewards are endless—for you, your partner, and your marriage. By the time you finish this book and complete the exercises, you will be a changed man, believing in the power of your sexuality.

Learn from Gary's sexual life.

Gary has always been comfortable expressing his sexuality. He is currently in his second marriage to Lisa, and they have a vibrant sex life. As sex holds significant importance for Gary, he wants to ensure it remains fulfilling.

Currently, Gary and Lisa engage in lovemaking almost every night and often in the mornings as well. For Gary, it's a routine activity akin to brushing his teeth—something done regularly throughout the day. However, Gary has started to notice that his "refractory period," the time between erections, is lengthening. He expresses concern, saying, "Lately, I can't always get it up twice a day." Gary is eager to discover new techniques that will enable him to continue enjoying extended periods of Intimacy with his wife, a sentiment shared by Lisa.

Arousal and Awareness

To know where you're going, you must first understand where you are. Regrettably, most men are not always conscious of their current feelings and experiences and have minimal awareness of their sexual responses. They are aware that something enjoyable is taking place, but they are unsure of the specifics. They are aware of their arousal, that much is certain, but they are unaware of the nuances of their own experience. This places significant restrictions on the male and his companion.

If a man knows how his body changes at different arousal levels, He will discover how to pay attention to the cues his body is sending him and how to use them to his advantage as well as his partner's benefit.

What Level of Aroused Are You?

What does the typical male say when you ask him whether he's feeling aroused? "Yes" or "No." What does he answer when you ask him to explain his level of arousal? Not much more than that. However, you'll have a completely different discussion about arousal if you ask a Multiorgasmic male about it.

Multi-orgasmic men are adept at controlling their arousal. They are aware of the subtleties of their sensual encounter and use their sensitivity to enhance and extend it. A multiorgasmic male will take at least five pages, single-spaced, to describe his excitement. Maybe even a poem thrown in.

In actuality, sexual arousal is a highly intricate and nuanced process. There are various arousal levels, and each has unique feelings and intensities. There are variations in intensity and degree; it's not a binary situation. It resembles a rainbow a lot more. Right now, our primary goal is to increase our awareness of the minute distinctions between each color of the rainbow so that we can recognize and enjoy them all.

You will have far closer ties to your own body as you become sensitized to your various arousal levels. When you begin to work with your body to achieve your first multiple orgasms, that becomes incredibly crucial. Being stimulated alone won't do if you want to have many orgasms. You have to be awake and conscious. It resembles learning how to compose music. Even though everything sounds good to you, writing a song requires knowledge of every note in the scale. It gets easier the more you hone your ear. Although they are more subdued, sharps and flats are just as significant. You will become as familiar with your arousal levels as a composer is with the notes of a scale by the time you have finished the tasks in this chapter. We're going to create an arousal scale of our own to make this easier.

Erection and Arousal

You'll see how Erections are not something I've discussed. Men frequently confuse arousal with erections, but the two are not the same. Arousal is a sensation; it is an individual's subjective feeling of excitement that is felt all over the body but usually feels most strong in the genitalia. On the other hand, erection describes the penis's firmness. A highly objective indicator of hardness, erection is a direct result of blood flow into this organ.

Even though a man is extremely excited, he may not be erect. Perhaps this is how you've felt after a long night of making love when your penis called it quits for the evening, but your mind was itching to go on. Maybe you experienced this with a new relationship that made you both incredibly excited and anxious. A lot of men have genuinely experienced being so stimulated that they had an orgasm, yet they were never erect.

Perhaps you reach full erection at arousal, or maybe erectness doesn't occur until you stir up yourself more. Or, possibly, like most males, it varies depending on the day. We won't be worrying too much about erections here, so it isn't essential at this time. Your degree of arousal is what we are worried about. You've undoubtedly already discovered from personal experience that trying to concentrate too much on your erection will actually make it less successful. However, if you leave it alone, it usually makes its way back home. Please don't consider it, then. All you have to do at this point is concentrate on your numbers.

Man and Woman Differences

It would be best if you gained some additional insight into your partner's workings so that you can both benefit from the encounter. Your partner might not always find success with what works for you. in the event that the two of you are pushing separate directions while attempting to sow a boat. You won't enjoy the journey, it will become really frustrating, and you won't get where you're going. To make this journey much more exciting, let's learn a little bit about how you can fulfill your partner and how they can satisfy you. Most of the time, men are eager for sex right away. And... when they're prepared for sexual activity, that's when it happens. Before they are ready for sexual activity, most women often need to engage in foreplay for at least fifteen minutes. This is not a choice or a habit. It is basically a function of their anatomy. It is time for us to learn about the opposing sex since we are not born knowing this information. I promise it will be of great use to you.

Foreplay

Most males associate sex with intercourse. Women are right when they say that having sex is simply one aspect of it.

Consider it in this manner if you were eager to view a fantastic film and truly desired to see it. If I came up to you and revealed the conclusion, how would you feel? Would you find the movie to be ruined by it? It will; you are sure of it. That's exactly how most women feel throughout a sexual encounter, thinking only of how gratifying every minute of the film is. The majority of guys typically spoil and reveal the outcome.

Not favorable. Let's make that adjustment.

Men can typically acquire an erection rapidly and are ready for sex right away. Before they are ready, most women need to engage in foreplay for at least fifteen minutes. A woman's clitoris and vagina do not become sufficiently stimulated and prepared for direct stimulation in the absence of foreplay.

Men should understand that they may enjoy foreplay just as much as women do. If only they try it with the tune.

Foreplay needs to be enjoyable in order to be effective. You need to be at ease and prepared to take full advantage of it. Men should remember to unwind and take deep ay even if they are typically eager to get to the end. This will make the sex that follows much more satisfying and passionate.

At this point, I should also mention that "Kissing" is one of the easiest and most effective ways to initiate a sexual encounter.

Women can also be told that fantastic sex is usually just around the corner by their partners through a beautiful kiss.

According to a lady, "If my partner wants to get me ready for sex, the best way to do it is with a long, slow, passionate kiss!"

Now, here are some pointers for increasing the excitement and enjoyment of foreplay:

Use your tongue, lips, fingers, and bands in as many creative ways as you can with your companions.

Sustain mystery for the other person.

To add to the sensation of unpredictability, vary the pressure, strokes, and speed of your touches.

Alternate between starting at the lips and going down in a straight line. Men should attempt a different approach, such as starting at the lips, moving to the neck, chest, stomach, and finally, the ears, if they typically begin at the lips and end up in the nether regions. Return to the lips next, and finally, the stomach. Recall that if your partner can anticipate your following action, things will usually get monotonous. Here's an additional recommendation: let's alter the habit of beginning with a lip kiss. The next time, start by giving your partner's hands and fingers a kiss. Alternately, begin from the feet and progress upward. Be playful, lighthearted, and erratic.

Try out various temps and textures. Apply creams, oils, feathers, ice cubes, silk scarves, and other items on each other's bodies. Variability is the crucial word here. If you're willing to be imaginative and receptive to new experiences, having sex won't ever get dull.

Share dessert. Try some watery fruits (strawberries, oranges, cantaloupe, etc.), chocolate ice cream, or even whipped cream. Alternatively, try eating or licking food off each other's bodies rather than feeding each other.

Providing one another with A delightful massage is another lovely way to engage in foreplay.

There are countless options. All you really need is some fun, adventure, and an open mind!

Male advice: Don't let the consensus that 15 minutes is sufficient to prepare a woman for sex limit you. You can definitely enjoy it for a lot longer. I trust you!

Prolonged Foreplay

Although it always makes for a more pleasurable encounter, foreplay is not limited to the moments right before intercourse.

You don't have to begin foreplaying immediately before intercourse. It may start days, weeks, or even hours before the significant event. Even if you live far apart, it might still begin. And you're going to adore it, I promise!

24 hours Foreplay

Make time for just the two of you during the day, and schedule sex for the very end.

Enjoy your favorite activities together, such as going on a picnic, riding a bike, shopping, or engaging in a hobby or favorite sport. Hugs and kisses are encouraged. Talk nasty, flirt, whisper in their ears, tease, and more. Don't do anything but have sex.

Express to one another how hot they make you feel. Express to each other how much you're anticipating and enjoying the evening. Even while it could be challenging to persevere through the entire day, the benefits will be well worth the wait. We should advise you that there might be property damage, clothing ripping, or both. When you demonstrate to a woman your lust for her, she will reciprocate! A woman will not only have the best foreplay she has ever had, but she will also have sex beyond your wildest expectations if you can genuinely convey to her how much she turns you on with your words and deeds.

When you're out in public, at a party, or any other kind of gathering, whisper in her ear. Inform her that the thought of seeing her nude tonight is all you can think about. Here, it's all about driving each other insane with your touch and words. It will be much more spectacular when you finally get to have sex. Women can make similar thoughts as by men.

Every time you gaze at each other, tell each other how insane they make you. Show each other that you can't sell them anything by touching each other in non-sales ways. Your spouse will demonstrate to you how wild they can go in bed if you can make them feel sexy, attractive, and wanted.

The same is true for women and men. Tell him just what you intend to do to him when you two are alone, whispering in his ear. Use as much imagery as necessary to convey your message. Recall that guys are primarily visual. The appropriate phrases will help you see them beforehand!

Just before bed, indulge in foreplay and turn each other on. When you're both about to climax, stop and call it a night. That's correct; we were hoping you could stop before you both have an orgasm and bid each other a good night. Make this arrangement in advance so that you are both aware of the strategy. Pick up where you left off the following morning when you awaken. While we don't promise that it will be simple, the sex that morning will be spectacular if you can make it through the night.

Kissing

The majority of guys view a kiss as a gateway to sex. They typically don't spend a lot of time on it because of this. For numerous ladies, a kiss is essential! It's also the best kind of foreplay, according to some. Kissing is also very, very crucial since most women require foreplay before they are ready for intercourse.

Go gradually and set the movies aside. While sometimes a passionate, furniture-destroying, clothe-ripping kiss is fantastic, for the majority of kisses, try the slow-motion variation. Your chances of obtaining mutual satisfaction are significantly higher.

As a general rule, kiss for at least five minutes before removing your clothes. The following advice can help you become a far better kisser:

- A kiss must begin slowly and with extreme tenderness.
- Don't kiss with your tongue in the first place.
- Let your lips brush each other very lightly at first, nearly to the point where it's difficult to tell if you're kissing or not.
- Increase the intensity very gradually while using light strokes and small nibbles.
- Using your tongue or the tip of your finger, gently and slowly circle the outside of the other person's lips as an excellent place to start, then begin the genuine kiss after that.
- When your tongues do eventually come into contact, it's still done sensually and delicately. Play with the tongue of the person opposite you.

Men can kiss a woman and gently sucking on her bottom lip. Savor the moment of kissing. Concern yourself with nothing but the now. Give each other an opportunity to return the kiss. And relish the sensation of that. Take turns taking the lead and the receiving one. Next, give the lead to the other person while you take it.

When you first kiss her, it's a good idea for guys to grasp her face with your hands lightly. Ladies adore that! It's seductive, romantic, and comforting all at once. Occasionally, during the kiss, men can also pull women up by her waist. She feels slender, seductive, and incredibly feminine as a result. Gently trace each other's faces and necks with your fingertips. For many, these are incredibly sensual and romantic.

Kiss her on the lips for a minimum of thirty seconds before extending your kiss to her neck or ears. Make sure to return to the lips after that. Keep in mind to be a little erratic.

Although it might seem apparent, this is frequently overlooked or forgotten. Males should kiss far more often during sexual activity than just before and after. And when you see her about to have an orgasm, kiss her. She will be left speechless by it.

Chapter 2

Couples Date Night

Nowadays, most people find the concept of organizing a date night to be highly intriguing and thrilling. Unfortunately, the majority of married couples are unaware of the value and relevance of this practice in maintaining a vibrant and stimulating marriage. It ought to be looked into as a potential activity to strengthen the union and establish a long-lasting, fruitful relationship.

Date Night

Here are a few creative ideas for creating exciting date nights that people can enjoy in order to maintain the spark in their marriage: Some people think that taking a little vacation to indulge in a quick retreat is thrilling and seductive. This could take the relatively cheap shape of the closest bed and breakfast in the area.

This will provide the couple the freedom to concentrate solely on each other, avoiding all the distractions that would typically demand their attention.

Couples Camp

Another affordable yet thrilling approach to reignite the sensual romance is to go camping or have dinner outside, which has frequently been shown to be the perfect romantic date night treat.

The couple can also refocus on one another and temporarily put everything else aside during this activity.

Couples Toast

Another excellent method to create a seductive date night is to select a bottle of wine that you both love and some dessert that is known to be seductive. Then, spend a quiet evening together, savouring these treats while getting to know each other's bodies and minds. When properly chosen, wine and dessert have frequently been shown to be the perfect combination to make people feel comfortable and content. Experience so forming the ideal frame of mind for the sensual date night pleasure.

Impress your partner with a passionate gesture.

When one makes an effort to offer a romantic gesture, it is typically warmly received by the recipient, and there is a good possibility that both parties will find the gesture's result to be mutually beneficial.

Adopt a romantic attitude.

Here are a few effortless and reasonably priced ways to set up situations where you can make romantic gestures toward the other person in an effort to charm them and keep the relationship going strong:

It's crucial to plan one date night into your weekly routine. If a weekly schedule is unfeasible, then at least two date nights each month should be agreed upon by both parties. The Date night should be treated seriously and should not be canceled carelessly once a commitment has been made. When the dates are kept on schedule, it would demonstrate the degree of interest on both sides. Significantly undervalued in terms of the sentimental act of genuinely dedicating some alone time so that the pair can have good communication.

Establishing a calm atmosphere that allows for a conversation to flow easily and without intimidation is a highly pleasurable exercise. When a couple can talk about subjects other than their everyday activities, they are typically able to see each other as fresh, exciting people who are self-assured and constantly changing. As a result, the likelihood of staleness is strongly avoided, and both parties become more conscious of and interested in making additional romantic gestures towards one another, helping to maintain the relationship's freshness factor.

Indulging in a full body massage for one another is another romantic gesture worth doing. This is less expensive and does not always require the knowledge of a masseuse. Both parties will be able to explore, unwind, and appreciate each other if they are able to extend this to one another.

Chapter 3

What, When, Where, and How for Couples Pleasure

Ignite the Moment by Activating some Activities.

Together with your partner, watch a scary movie. Research indicates that individuals, particularly females, often confuse emotions of dread with those of being aroused. Okay, this is useful! Don't allow the arousal factor go to waste after you've watched a scary movie together. You could even wish to make a film of your own. Of course, for private screening only.

Together, watch a mature film. Yes, we are aware that ladies aren't meant to appreciate this to the same extent as men. When you view an adult film together again, see how many different postures you can identify. Take a look at the elegant ones. Of course, it's okay if you have to watch it by yourself. Don't forget to take notes. You might now need to attempt viewing a romantic movie together in order to balance things out. Yes, I can hear the folks at the rear jeering. In any case, give it a shot.

Additionally, while you're watching, hold hands, cuddle up in each other's arms, and perhaps even share a kiss or two. But hold off on hefty stuff till after the film. After that, make every effort possible.

Together, work out. Your libido tends to rise along with your stamina as you exercise. It also improves the efficiency of all your systems, including the sexual ones. Longer and more pleasurable sex is the result.

Engage in a game or sport that requires a lot of holding and touching between you. A round of nude Twister, perhaps? Shower together as a couple. Can water be saved with this as well? Indeed. The crucial query here is, though: who gets to pick up the soap off the floor next? Together, take a hot bath or shower. Gently and sensually slough each other off. All the erogenous zones (chest/breasts, buttocks, stomach, back, back of neck, inner thighs, etc.) should receive more attention.

Offer to massage her scalp and wash her hair. Whoops, someone unintentionally dropped the soap. One of you needs to go down on your knees, please. If you're interested in that kind of stuff, you could even try looking for the soap while you're down there.

Together, read sultry bedtime stories. Ask her to lend you one of her romance novels if you are unable to locate any. If she doesn't have any, you can identify a whole row of these titles in any major bookstore. They range from serious porn to lighthearted romance. Choose what you want. Engage in obscene conversation with one another. Take it gently at first and discover what suits the two of you.

Engage in mutual masturbation to strengthen your understanding of how to achieve greater satisfaction during sexual activity and to grow closer as a couple.

Weekend afternoon naps should be taken. Oral sex can be used to wake up the other person, whichever wakes up first. To avoid any surprises or strangeness, talk about this and the concept in advance. It might not suit every person. If that's too much for one of you, then just use your hands and/or tongue for massage or slow, gentle fondling. Instead, wake each other up in this manner.

There is a lot of foreplay in dance. The smell of colognes and/or fragrances mixed with breathing, gentle touching, and proximity can work wonders.

Make a dance while wearing only your underwear. Not the ones you wear when doing laundry, please. Try something seductive and sensual. Something similar to International Male and Victoria's Secret. Play any game that has the term "strip" attached to it, such as strip poker. This is a game where there are no losers. On a hike, take a "quickie" break. It's also a lot of fun to go camping, so bring a good tent. Somehow, being in nature makes people think about having sex. Check to see whether it awakens your inner animal!

Here are some pointers for overcoming the "time" obstacle along with a few extra benefits: Make an unexpected call to your partner and arrange a "lunch" rendezvous. In fact, just have dessert right away and skip lunch. Is that what's referred to as a nooner? Get up one to two hours earlier than usual. For both men and women, the morning is when sex hormones peak. When is the best moment to enjoy passionate, steamy, and sweaty sex? After, if you're still feeling energetic, take a shower together. Showering in sex isn't limited to mornings, either. It could be beneficial at any time. Go to bed thirty minutes sooner than normal. Now that we have an extra half hour, what could we do? No, we didn't intend to watch TV, unless there was a sexy moment.

Decide to play chess when you wake up in the middle of the night. Alternatively, you might just have amazing sex. It's your decision. Whoever wakes up first gets to experience the benefit of waking the other person up with just their hands and tongue. Use your imagination. Consider everything you do in a day and how you could combine those activities. Lunches and showers are just the start. You will never again remark to yourself, I don't have time for sex.

Is Sex Limited to Bedroom?

Building on the idea that change drives off boredom, establish a clear guideline from the outset: You are to have sex someplace other than the bedroom as often as possible. This straightforward rule can lead to many inventive options, such as using the kitchen table, coffee table, bathtub, shower, rocking chair, gym equipment, wall, or the floor of every room in the house. That only applies "inside the house." What about the garage, the backyard, the inside of the car, the car's hood, or the outdoors while camping, hiking, or having a picnic? For that matter, you can liven things up in any public space.

A special spark and thrill are added to sex when it takes place in an area where there is a chance of being discovered. Try the stairway, the host's bedroom during a party, the swimming pool, sneaking away from your parents after supper, your office at work (or an empty office, or even your boss's office!) Some have even ventured into the aircraft lavatory. However, you take all of this danger. Please don't blame us if you are discovered.

A romantic hotel package or even a motel room could be rented. Go on a cruise together or rent a timeshare or cabin in a different nation, state, or city. We have a ton of recommendations to get you going.

Anything, though, will do to change things up and prevent boredom! Let's say you are teenagers experiencing your first sexual encounter. All you have to do is invest a little time and effort into coming up with new ideas and locations to work. The rest will be provided by your brain. Entering the domain of fantasy is enjoyable for certain individuals as well. Meet each other in a pub and act as though you are going on a first date. Alternatively, attempt to embrace each other as though you've just recently met. Viewers will find it entertaining as well. But unless you want to spend the night at good ol' Fido's house, don't leave the bar with anybody else.

Learn New styles

Improving your technique does not just entail understanding the mechanics of new techniques, it also means being flexible enough to adapt moves you already know to different events, moods, and moments. Once more, the main goal is to eliminate boredom and to avoid being ordinary as much as possible. Being exceptional is your aim – Recall that diversity is an essential term. As previously stated, if you have sex in the same settings, with the same style, and in the same positions, The sizzle fades every time. There's no mystery or spirit of adventure. It is foreseeable. It is monotonous. Simply put, it's not enjoyable. Men can also typically be prepared for sexual activity right away, as was previously said. Women often require at least fifteen minutes of foreplay. Simply put, that's how the bodies of men and women differ. Recognize it and find a way to accommodate it.

There are differences between men and women. Men typically target a woman's genitalia first since it is what they would want to see. They're prepared now! And they think women operate in the same way. Women typically agree to it. Typically, they don't provide verbal or physical input to fix the error—likely to preserve the masculine ego. Ultimately, the majority of men believe they are adept at winning over ladies. Women, meanwhile, do not approach a man's genitals immediately. Indeed, they will come into contact with till the man eventually takes her hand and puts it on, he touches him everywhere else than her genitalia. She's kissing and caressing him in a way that makes her feel good. She wants to be caressed. She believes that he will experience the same happiness as she does. Thus, How can this be fixed?

For Men

Men should take it more slowly. Touch her all over except her clitoris and vagina, at least briefly first ten to fifteen minutes. Women's bodies are covered in hot spots and erogenous zones. Play them all and have fun with them all. A woman's body is an artistic creation. If only she had the time to let you know all, value everything. When you eventually reach to the vaginal area, avoid contacting her directly to truly aggravate her. Tease her on the clitoris or vagina. Caress her all around the opening of her vagina including the inner thighs, beneath the vagina, etc. When she finally gives up on it completely, Touch the primary areas gradually. By employing this playful method, you might occasionally be able to get her to climax because the intensity has been built up. This is an other perspective on things... Observe how males consume ice cream. Usually, they can be completed in an instant. Right now, saw ladies enjoying ice cream. The majority of them will take their time, relish every molecule. They'll use it to make fun of themselves, put it in their mouths, and shut. As it melts on the tip of the tongue, close your eyes and imagine yourself in heaven. Well, huh. .... That's how they define enjoyment.

Consequently, although quickies and nooners play a role, in most for them, cases are the dessert that they may savor for extended periods of time. Why should I do all this for her? It is a question you may be wondering.

Well, for starters, you're reading this book to improve your ability om bed. Right? Alright. If a rationale is still required, Here's a fantastic one: If you can truly make a woman feel good in bed and completely satisfy her, She will return the favor by tenfold in pleasure! Sufficient for you.

Now let's go on.

The majority of males begin by kissing the lips, then the neck, the breasts, the stomach, and finally When they reach the end zone, they set up camp. It is foreseeable. She is aware of your exact next move every time you play the same film once more. She anticipates that you will begin at her lips and descend quickly in a line, sharing a kiss or two along the way. The easiest route to boredom is that. Given that erogenous zones can be found across the body, strike each one, then switch them out. Use various rhythms, speeds, and strokes, and maintain her speculations. Wherever you would ordinarily zag, zig. Keep her guessing. This is a brief illustration of what you could do: Gently stroke her crotch with your hand as you give her a kiss on the lips. The underwear is still on. While doing so, shift your lips from kissing her lips to kissing her neck and then her bosom. Then, push her aside and return to her lips. and finally, to her stomach. Slowly, brush your lips over her pubic hair. Then return to her breasts. The enigma and capriciousness will make her insane! It will activate her, and once you reach her vagina, both of you will find it much more enjoyable! Try a different version of the above the next time. Begin with something new. Try varied angles and thrust speeds, try new positions, and move away from the bed. Attempt The couch or the chair. Sometimes a new approach is just an application of an old technique to a new theme or setting.

Stimulation directly

Avoid making direct movements when you're stimulating her clitoris with your hands or mouth. Rather, softly massage the hood and the clitoris' folds. for a brief moment. Next, progressively reveal the head and make gentle circular movements with your finger or tongue. concerning the clitoris. As soon as you sense that she's about to have an orgasm, begin massaging the clitoris straight, but use extreme caution. Additionally, confirm that there is sufficient lubrication or it will cause her pain. When she starts to experience an orgasm, return to stroking her in the clitoris rather than stimulating directly. Her orgasm will cause the clitoris to become extremely sensitive and direct touch can cause pain.

Multiple Orgasm

After getting to climax, it's best to slow down in order to offer her many orgasms. Avoid touching the clitoris directly. Give her some time to gather her thoughts, then continue by applying semi-direct contact or clitoris stimulation to her once more.

Typically, she'll have another orgasm in the next two to five minutes. As she's having an orgasm, give her a kiss on the lips to truly make her gasp.

For Females

In response, women are able to slightly accelerate. You might give him a kiss on the neck, chest, and stomach, and at the sides for a little period of time before engaging the penis. As you're sharing a kiss, you can feel the material of his pants rubbing against his crotch. Generally speaking, men enjoy a bit more pressured than women while stroking and petting. Next, insert your hand into his pants and follow suit. Proceed to caress the penis with your hand. Rub gently against and rub his scrotum. As long as you treat it gently, it won't break. You are able to even give them a light squeeze—not too forceful, though. The idea is to keep the male interested in you as you extend the foreplay. Men require immediate, direct touch, thus doing this will satisfy him while you're on a path to complete arousal. For more pleasure, add this step while stimulating the penis. As you were petting the penis, gently grasp the scrotum with your other hand. Next, as you keep stroking the penis, use the other hand to gently and slowly massage the scrotum. It will be adored by him.

Use the Method of Milking;

Squeeze his penis just before he goes into an orgasm. This typically makes the orgasms. If you're stroking with your hand, squeeze around the penis. Squeeze your vaginal walls during sexual activity to get the same result. This method is effective and easy for the woman to squeeze when she is on top.

In the traditional ' woman on top' pose, the woman sits over him and the male lies on his back. The lady can regulate the thrusts' angle and speed more effectively, and can so more readily experience an orgasm. Usually, the man lies on his back, and this delay ejaculation. This position's modified variant benefits both parties better. Rather than adopting an erect posture, The woman can bend forward at any angle between 45 and 60 degrees, using her hands to provide stability. Then, she slides her hips backward rather than forward. and so on. The woman can experience increased clitoral stimulation in this posture, which further prolongs the man's life in comparison to the up-and-down motion. The woman can utilize her hair to brush against the man's chest when she is in the lead. more enjoyment. Additionally, women might collaborate with their male partners to help them slow down and even endure longer. Later in this chapter, there are some pointers provided. The finest method to make your partner love sex is the last but most significant piece of advice for women. To put it simply, more means more sex. Reiterating the guidance that women should take the lead is beneficial. Have more sex! Your sexual life will significantly improve just by taking this one step.

Acquire Mutual Knowledge

Similar to how you can please one another by just doing the opposite of what you used to do. Moreover, you can also get additional knowledge about how to fulfill one another's needs in other domains. By showing each other this kind of sharing and interest in your mate, you can improve as lovers different. Express to one another what you both think makes the ideal kiss. Exchange kisses in turns, but The other person just appreciates your kiss and is unable to return it. Next, swap. This will manifest You may mimic how the other person prefers to be kissed by knowing exactly how they do it. While the other observes and makes mental notes, masturbate in front of each other. Eventually, the onlooker can participate as well by giving a few simple touches or kisses. This will be beneficial. You both gain a great deal of knowledge about fulfilling one another. This approach may initially cause discomfort for some individuals. But get over it. since doing so will also deepen your Intimacy and bond between the two of you. Consequently, this will enhance the pleasure and delight of having sex.

Without having sex, try to get each other on climax. Utilize just your lips and hands and tongue. Or, for today, just use your hands. And tomorrow, just your tongue and lips will do. When necessary, the individual being satisfied can give verbal or physical feedback.

How can a man Last longer?

A common grievance expressed by both genders is that men have a tendency to have orgasms far more quickly than women. The bad news is that one of these men might be you. The good news is that this kind of issue is somewhat typical. There are others besides you. The fact that the issue is fixable is wonderful news. Men can lengthen their staying duration with these two easy methods:

1. Start and Stop

In order to use this technique, the man must touch his penis until he feels close to experience an orgasm. After that, cease stroking, inhale deeply, and then breathe out slowly. Continue breathing until the desire to reach a peak is gone. Proceed again after that. The man will be able to better control his orgasms thanks to this method. Once he can manage his orgasms, the following stage is to attempt the same method using grease. Replicating the sensations of real sexual activity is the aim here. This procedure will be more challenging than the last one. He can advance to employing this after mastering the use of lubricant to control orgasms. He can use the method during sexual activity. Men have learned to survive for as long as they use this 'start and stop' approach to postpone their orgasms and have the sex they want.

2. Kegel Exercises

One more method to postpone ejaculation and prolong sex is to perform Kegel exercises. It's accomplished by tensing and relaxing your pubococcygeus muscles. To find your pubococcygeus muscles, attempt moving your penis without your hands. Your pubococcygeus muscles are the ones used for this. Additionally, you employ these muscles to prevent yourself from urinating.

The typical guy's muscles are insufficient to prevent ejaculation. But like any other muscle, they can become stronger with exercise and more powerful such that they aid ejaculation control. Just tense these muscles, hold them for a moment, then release the tension. Next, carry out the procedure. Work your way up to as many repetitions as you can in a session by starting again after 50 rounds. These can be performed anywhere, even in the comfort of your vehicle.

Sitting in your workplace and browsing the internet, or waiting for the light to change. Nobody will be aware of it. You can perform these every day, once or twice. If you experience any pain or discomfort, take a rest for the following day and carry on.

Similar to any other workout, don't overdo it and start out slowly. The majority of guys experience benefits in one to three months. It might not be after the first three months. Kegel exercises must be performed daily. However, keep working out the pubococcygeus muscles to keep the strength from time to time. It's fantastic if you can manage to do it every day. It's time to exercise your more powerful pubococcygeus muscles now. When you sense that an orgasm is approaching, tighten your PC muscles by clamping. Hold till the need to ejaculate reaches one minute. and then gradually let the muscles relax. Take a long, deep breath out as you unwind. Repeat the process again and again . You can essentially stay in bed for as long as you want if you have strong pubococcygeus muscles. If you finally ejaculation, it will be significantly stronger and you will experience orgasms greater intensity.

Chapter 4

The Advantages of a Strong Sexual Life to Your Marriage

There are a number of reasons why sex seems to be so important in marriages, and those who want to keep the "spark" alive should really consider the advantages of excellent sex and how it affects the structure of the marriage.

Some common advantages that arise from a couple being able to have a satisfying sexual relationship within the confines of marriage include the following:

Having sex contributes to calorie burn.

Although most people would consider having sex to be an absurd method of burning calories—especially since the gym is typically where calorie-burning exercises are associated with this need—sex is also known to yield comparable results and to be a more natural means of becoming and remaining agile and in shape.

An additional advantage of having a fulfilling sexual life in marriage is that it keeps the couple closer and more intimate, which fosters the creation of a warm, ideal family that is welcoming and comfortable for all members of the family.

Increased Emotional Intimacy

Regular sexual activity can strengthen the emotional bond between partners, leading to a more profound sense of connection and

41

closeness. Our bodies release oxytocin, also known as the love hormone, during sexual activity. This hormone promotes attachment, trust, and bonding. Your relationship with your spouse can become more emotionally intense if you both consistently feel these good feelings. Furthermore, having sex can be a sensitive act that calls for confidence and safety in your relationship. The emotional relationship is strengthened when this vulnerability is treated with consideration and dignity. Even in the absence of sexual activity, physical connection during sex, such as holding hands or snuggling, releases oxytocin. These displays of affection facilitate feelings of Intimacy and emotional connection.

Improved Communication

Couples who engage in healthy sexual activity often find it easier to communicate openly and honestly about their needs, desires, and concerns.

A couple can feel more relaxed and comfortable if there are frequent, satisfying sex encounters. This can facilitate candid and frank discussions, including ones concerning sex. In a relationship, a robust sexual connection can contribute to a feeling of safety and stability. Partners can feel free to express themselves and their needs in this secure area. No matter how much we may work to value a relationship's physical aspects, communication is unquestionably essential to fostering closeness and creating solid, healthy sexual bonds. Sexual satisfaction is higher in couples who are able to express their feelings and wishes to each other honestly than in those who are unable to do so. In order to establish a close relationship between two people, communication is essential for anything from setting limits to encouraging candid discussions about wants and expectations.

Greater Sense of Security

Knowing that their sexual needs are being met can create a sense of security and stability in the relationship.

Increased Relationship Longevity

Research suggests that couples who maintain a satisfying sexual relationship are more likely to stay together in the long term.

Overall, a solid sexual life can contribute to a healthier, happier, and more fulfilling marriage for both partners.

Great sex does teach both partners to be less self-centered and more giving; this attitude carries over into other areas of the couple's lives as well, where they are more inclined to give and take rather than always taking or expecting to be the recipient.

In addition, it supports a more whole and healthy state of mind and body for the person.

Frequent sexual activity is beneficial for the heart and reduces stress in all people, making it an excellent method of stress relief.

Chapter 5

The Advent of Male Multiple Orgasm for Sexual Pleasure

Male Multiple orgasms are the term used to describe the ability of certain men to experience several orgasms in a short amount of time without going through the refractory period, which is the period of recovery following an orgasm during which it is not physiologically feasible to experience more orgasms. This is not the case for the typical male sexual reaction, which frequently consists of a refractory phase that prevents more orgasms.

Learning specialized methods, such as those used in some Tantra or Taoist sexual practices, is usually necessary to achieve numerous orgasms. In order to postpone ejaculation and extend pleasure, these methods frequently center on managing arousal levels, breathing patterns, and muscular contractions. It's important to remember that different men have different experiences and that not all men are able to have many orgasms.

Some women want to have hours-long sex sessions, while others prefer brief, straightforward Intimacy. A typical woman's demands and aspirations vary depending on the day.

How about understanding your partner's differences? What is her likes and dislikes? what is her want? and how might her needs change from day to week? You should be aware of this information. That's the only way your newly discovered talents will genuinely benefit the two of you. If not, you can be engaging in a variety of activities in which your spouse has no interest.

Try to Understand me. Your requirements are significant. However, you have to always keep in mind that your partner's demands are just as substantial. Nothing is more annoying than a man who is simply going about his business without considering what the lady actually wants. It takes more than simply awareness of your own body to be an excellent lover. Being a great lover also entails understanding your partner's body and, perhaps more importantly, understanding her thinking. Being multiorgasmic has the advantage of offering you a level of sexual flexibility that you have never known. You can experience extreme pleasure for the first time without compromising your partner's requirements in the slightest. Not only will your experience be far more intense than hers, but you'll contribute to hers being even more intense. While you are taking care of yourself admirably, you are also able to take care of her in ways that you have never been able to. Nobody has to give up a lot or accept a low-quality product.

I've heard women lament over indifferent men who don't appear to care about what they truly need or about men who aren't able to commit. However, I have to admit that I have never heard a woman lament a man who could provide her with anything she wanted. It's crucial that you and your spouse discuss your requirements during your talks, but it's perhaps even more vital to discuss hers. Allow her to express her desires and dislikes to you. Does she feel uneasy about anything? Does she have any fears? Please pay close attention to her responses and refrain from making any assumptions. You might be shocked to learn that you don't know as much as you think about your spouse. I strongly advise you to seize this fantastic chance to show your concern and get closer to each other. If your spouse is asking a lot of questions regarding her particular role in your "training," going through the book with her should provide the answers she seeks. You'll see that the roles of men and women are always discussed in detail as you go through each couple exercise (some don't even need a partner). Even in the event that the woman chooses not to engage in any of the activities, I strongly advise that both couples read the book.

Since every woman is unique, I cannot possibly predict how your partner will react to anything I discuss. In my opinion, I hope she wishes to approach this as a sort of cooperative venture. I say this because I have seen firsthand how much more exciting things are for both couples when a woman is involved in the process. But as I've already stated, a woman merely needs to be there at the finish line, grinning broadly, to support her man in learning these new skills.

How Possible Is Multiple Orgasm for Male?

Some guys, especially those in their youth, are just naturally fortunate. These men are born athletes. Because of the way their bodies work, they either never lose their erections after an orgasm, or they regain them so fast that they hardly even last during sexual activity. This kind of man is "born" multiorgasmic. Perhaps this was a fortunate moment in your own life as well. However, likely, such times are over. The good news is that becoming multiorgasmic no longer requires luck. There is an alternative method to learn this skill, and it applies to all ages, backgrounds, and divinely endowed abilities.

Being multiorgasmic actually has an effortless secret. For the majority of men who have perfected the art, the key is understanding how to experience a whole orgasm devoid of ejaculation. Yes, a full-blown, potent orgasm without ejaculation—or two, or three, or more. There would be no refractory period and no downtime without ejaculation. This implies that your erection won't significantly diminish, allowing you to carry on having sex until you're ready for an orgasm and simultaneous ejaculation.

I understand that this might not sound as easy as I say it is. It's likely that everything seems incredibly strange or perhaps unfeasible right now. I understand that in comparison to most men, As far as orgasms are concerned, they cannot exist without ejaculation.

Like thunder and lightning, it comes as a package, right? False. Although it may seem unlikely, most sex therapists would attest that orgasm and ejaculation in men are two different things. Sure, they usually happen in tandem, and sure, it does seem like a package deal. However, in terms of physiology, they are not inseparable. The secret to being multiorgasmic is realizing that it is possible to have an orgasm in its entirety without also ejaculating simultaneously. Once you figure out how to separate them, you'll be good to go. I am aware that not every male reading this book at the moment finds this news to be astounding. Numerous males have inadvertently come across this. Indeed, there might have been one or more instances in your past where you felt the orgasmic sensations without really ejaculating.

You might not have given it much attention at the time, or you might have found it baffling. When this happens inadvertently, most guys assume it's an accident or some weird peculiarity.

While many men worry that they could be flawed, very few consider it a worthwhile experience to recreate, much less perfect. If you did, you most likely wouldn't be reading this book at this moment—instead, you would be using it. However, I can assure you that there are countless men I know who would be happy to tell you that having a non-sexual orgasm is an experience that should be relished and refined.

How to attain Multiple Orgasm?

1. You should locate your pubococcygeus muscle first and foremost. This is very easy for certain men to find—you probably already knew where to look for it when I brought it up. Maybe you're even sucking it at the now. However, a lot of men have no idea what muscles are in this part of the body. It's possible for every muscle near the abdomen, thighs, PC, and buttocks to feel the same. It could feel like they are all one large muscle mass. That has to change immediately. The easiest method for locating your pubococcygeus muscle and isolating it from the others is as follows. Put one or two fingers softly behind your testicles to start. Act as though you're peeing. Try to halt the flow now. Your PC muscle is the one you just employed to stop the bladder's flow. Did you sense it getting tighter? Perhaps you also observed that when you flexed your pubococcygeus, your testicles and penis "jumped" a little. It's critical that the muscles in your thighs and tummy stay calm. Did they also become tense? Give it another go. This time, pay attention to the pubococcygeus alone.

2. This is the next exercise to do once you've identified your PC muscle: Flex the PC twenty times a day, three times a day. Each time, hold it for a brief moment or two before letting go. And that's it. Twice a day, twenty squeezes. Though it may seem easy, there

are no enough words to convey the significance of this activity. For three weeks, I want you to perform this exercise three times a day, every day.

3. However, you will now add ten very gradual squeezes. You act in this manner. Squeeze your PC as tightly as you can for five seconds. Now, if you can, hold the strain for the whole five seconds. In the final five seconds, gradually relieve the strain. You ought to be able to feel the muscle being worked hard.

4. Caress her genitalia slowly, touching the exterior and interior of her vagina with your fingers or mouth. Apply a lot of lubricant. Give the areas you are touching your full attention. Take great note of their appearance and how they make you feel. Give yourself over to those feelings. Recall that this is an exercise without demands. You're not caressing her to win her over or arouse her interest. To make you happy, you are touching. Her pressure is released, and your pressure is released as well.

5. 5. Take a comfortable position on your back, close your eyes, and make yourself comfy (you could even want to sit in a cozy chair). Apply a generous amount of lubricant and softly, lightly caress your own body. Given that both of your thighs and nipples are presumably rather sensitive, you might want to start by touching them. Next, proceed gradually to the genitalia. Do not utilize a masturbating stroke after you start petting your penis. Avoid

attempting to sex yourself. Examine each fold and crease in the vaginal region. Give it some time.

6. Once more, you must take a seat or lie down and make yourself quite comfortable. Apply lubricant to your hand and genitalia. Now, using the technique you learned in Exercise 5, begin by gently caressing your genitalia until you achieve what you would consider to be a Level 4 of excitement. That means you've progressed past the "twinge" stage and are now experiencing a constant, low-pitched "hum" of arousal. Recall that you are petting yourself, not engaging in a masturbating gesture.

7. You should become comfortable, close your eyes, and lie on your back. The activity will start with a sensual concentrated genital caress from your partner. She ought to take her time and concentrate on enjoying herself. She can speak with her mouth, her hands, or both. You should only pay attention to your feelings. This relieves the strain on the two of you.

8. Take a comfortable seat or lie down, and start a genital self-care routine with lots of lubrication. As you slowly and gently stroke your penis, allow your level of arousal to gradually build.

9. Peaking with the PC muscle is an excellent pair exercise. Start by lying on your back and making yourself comfortable. Start a genital caress with your lover after using lots of lubricant. She can be stimulated orally or manually, depending on her preference. Recall that she is giving you a caress out of pure enjoyment. Squeeze your

PC muscle when you achieve a Level 4 on your arousal scale. Draw in a deep, long breath. Your spouse has not ceased the stimulation, but your PC squeeze should prevent your arousal from rising more. You can even get demoted by one level. You may tell when your spouse should cease caressing you by taking a deep breath. She shouldn't stop till your long breath is about to expire. Give yourself a two-level drop in arousal. You are prepared to proceed after you are optimistic that you have reached Level 2. Tell your lover she's welcome to resume her caresses. You will reach your peak at Level 6 this time. Squeeze your PC muscle when you get to Level 6. Draw in a deep, long breath. Your partner should cease all stimulation at the end of this breath and allow you to return to Level 4.

10. The majority of your weight will be supported by your hips and knees when you kneel between her legs. You're going to insert your penis now and start gently and slowly thrusting. It's never too sluggish to exercise this way. Rolling or swaying your pelvis will allow you to insert and remove your penis from her vagina. Keep your muscles relaxed. This is still an exercise in sensitive focus without pressure. Imagine yourself gently petting your partner's vagina with your penis. Pay attention to the feelings. Remain in the present moment. Avoid thinking about how you performed. This is only for your enjoyment. If you find your thoughts wandering, gently refocus on the enjoyable experiences you are currently having.

11. Applying a good deal of lubricant, start pecking at your penis. You should begin to feel more aroused. Utilizing the pubococcygeus muscle, Increase your stimulation and reach a peak after you have lowered a few levels. Once more, manage your peak with your pubococcygeus muscle. Give it some time. It should take at least fifteen or twenty minutes to get to your peaks.

This is where you are going to really push the peaking workout. Re-intensify your stimulation. Stop your arousal from rising by using your pubococcygeus muscle. To accomplish this, you must have a strong sense of bodily control. Now, when you're almost at the peak, there's a strong temptation to give in to temptation and have an orgasm. Please persevere if you can. Now, it won't be long. Your ultimate peak will occur when ejaculation feels inevitable—that is when you reach the psychological point of no return. Imagine dancing on a volcano. There is no peak like this one that you will ever climb.

Right now, you have to be completely aware of your body. You will be giving your penis a vigorous stroke, directly leading to ejaculation. However, you want to hit the pubococcygeus muscle as soon as you reach your point of inevitable—not a second later, but right then and there. Maintain the same speed at which you have been stroking your penis. Draw in a deep breath. Now open and maintain the opening of your eyes. Try to clench your pubococcygeus muscle for ten seconds or so.

www.ingramcontent.com/pod-product-compliance
Lightning Source LLC
Chambersburg PA
CBHW051245120626
46547CB00014B/1808